T0198969

KATHERINE HOWELLS

100
LOVE
MESSAGES

From The Love That Is Always Present

Copyright © 2023 Katherine Howells.

All rights reserved. No part of this book may be used or reproduced by any means, graphic, electronic, or mechanical, including photocopying, recording, taping or by any information storage retrieval system without the written permission of the author except in the case of brief quotations embodied in critical articles and reviews.

Balboa Press books may be ordered through booksellers or by contacting:

Balboa Press
A Division of Hay House
1663 Liberty Drive
Bloomington, IN 47403
www.balboapress.com
844-682-1282

Because of the dynamic nature of the Internet, any web addresses or links contained in this book may have changed since publication and may no longer be valid. The views expressed in this work are solely those of the author and do not necessarily reflect the views of the publisher, and the publisher hereby disclaims any responsibility for them.

Any people depicted in stock imagery provided by Getty Images are models, and such images are being used for illustrative purposes only.
Certain stock imagery © Getty Images.

ISBN: 979-8-7652-3642-0 (sc)
ISBN: 979-8-7652-3641-3 (e)

Library of Congress Control Number: 2022921189

Print information available on the last page.

Balboa Press rev. date: 12/15/2022

BALBOA.PRESS
A DIVISION OF HAY HOUSE

CONTENTS

Dedicated to The Messenger
and all those who see and celebrate the message

Love Generators

Love is alive,
each one of us
the bull's eye
on love's target.
Pierced to the very
center and source
by the generous
energy of love,
there is no other
course but to
become love
generators, little
dynamos radiating
the truth of love
in all its infinite
disguises.

Danna Faulds

I consider each of the images in this book a love generator. My deepest desire is that they touch you in a profound way, opening your heart to the true nature of Love.

Cotyledon in my garden

The first heart I remember noticing and photographing was a sweet little cotyledon.* The heart, the symbol of Love, seems to be the perfect image for this nourishing, selfless seed leaf.

It also seems a bit magical to me that the definition for cotyledon is: *an embryonic leaf in seed-bearing plants, one or more of which are the first leaves to appear from a germinating seed.*

Perhaps this first image of the cotyledon is like the first leaves, hinting at what is to come. What has germinated, and is now being nourished? What is to be learned about the true nature, the essence, of Love?

*cot·y·le·don
/ˌkädəˈlēdn/

*noun*BOTANY
noun: **cotyledon**; plural noun: **cotyledons**
an embryonic leaf in seed-bearing plants, one or more of which are the first leaves to appear from a germinating seed.

(1) Read more at Gardening Know How: What Is A Cotyledon: When Do Cotyledons Fall Off https://www.gardeningknowhow.com/garden-how-to/propagation/seeds/what-is-a-cotyledon.htm

What do we do when Love presents itself?

What do I do?

I take photographs

INTRODUCTION

I ask myself, 'what if?' What if Spirit is speaking to us all the time? What if we just don't notice because we are scurrying from one place to another, totally distracted by the thoughts in our heads? What if Spirit wanted to communicate something to us somewhat "dense" humans on this earth? How would Spirit do this? Perhaps by sending messages in the language that we can understand. When I see a heart, I think of Love. Love with a capital L symbolizes more than romantic love; that is included, but when you see the word Love with a capital L in this book, it means the Loving Presence that we can see and feel all around us. I believe it is this Presence that is demonstrating Itself through these images.

I've often had a sense that this Presence is communicating all the time through the natural world, it's just that most of us humans have forgotten how to listen. We've forgotten that the Universe speaks in a language different from our own learned language. In my experience, the natural world speaks through symbolic messages. These symbolic messages are easy to miss if we're not paying attention. Often, a lot of time passes when I am not very present to what's going on around me.

This book began birthing itself about seven years ago. My husband and I had recently moved from our home in the suburbs outside of Portland, Oregon, to 27 acres of land in the country where we wanted to retire. We began building a new life as caretakers of the land and the animals that began showing up.

The fact that we ended up on this farm after we retired is a bit ironic. I grew up on a farm in Oregon, and when I left there at 17 years of age to go to college, I didn't think I'd ever go back to farm life. It seems there may be some truth to the saying, "you can take the girl out of the country, but you can't take the country out of the girl." Growing up I had so much freedom to roam the land, and that is where I developed a very strong sense of connection with the natural world. In my later years, the land began calling me home.

My path back to the land occurred during an intense time of spiritual and personal growth. I began to see that I was carrying old patterns, habits, and ways of being that were not in alignment with my desire to be a more loving presence in the world. I began asking Spirit to show me what Love is. In place of Spirit, insert the word God/Universe/Creator if you so choose. I am using these terms interchangeably. In my opinion, they're all just words that don't come close to describing the Creative Loving Presence I'm referring to here in these pages. It is this Presence that I was listening for when I asked that my heart be opened to the true nature of Love.

The symbol of Love that most humans recognize is a heart. Shortly after I prayed to be shown what Love is, I began seeing hearts! Lots and lots of hearts! I saw them everywhere.

When I started photographing these hearts, I made a promise to myself that I would not change anything about the heart offering to try and make it more interesting, more photogenic, or more appealing in any way. I also decided not to enhance or edit these photos. This is not a photography book. I took these images with what was right there with me - my phone. I promise you that I did not create any of these images consciously. While some are made by my own hand, I only noticed them after the creation of them. In that sense, these are all "found" images and came to me with an element of surprise and delight.

Some of these images, especially those that were created by my own hand, are very every-day, mundane images, and you might ask, "what's so great about that?" If this comes up for you, I am asking you to remember that these images weren't consciously created. I didn't peel a vegetable with the thought that I would create a heart. I was just going about my daily business, doing my thing, and what "appeared" was a heart. It was an "accident". Or perhaps not. I ask myself, is life really all that mundane? What would our lives be like if we were really noticing what is around us?" What delights are we missing when we aren't present to what's right in front of us? I believe the images in this book are an attempt to answer that question.

Some of the messages may bring a little experience of "ew" to your senses. I did think about only including the more pleasant images, but then I realized that this is what life is…… beautiful at times, downright ugly and messy at times, and just plain mundane at times, so I've included the seemingly beautiful, the seemingly ugly, and the seemingly mundane.

This book is a sharing of these messages with you. There is a brief description of each image, and some narrative about what I've been learning in this process of discovery, but mostly I will let the photos speak for themselves. A few of the images demand a little longer story.

As these hearts continued to come over a period of several years, I have been reflecting upon the deeper meaning of them. Why are these showing up for me now? If it is Spirit responding to my prayer to show me what Love is, what is here for me to learn about Love?

It is my hope that this book conveys what I continue to learn. It seems only natural that these images of Love are presenting themselves in how life shows up, because I'm discovering that there is only Love for us here, no matter what we might believe or think we are seeing as we journey through this sacred gift of life.

As I said, I didn't write this book. When the hearts started showing up, I noticed them, and I began photographing them. I had no idea they would keep coming. After several years of witnessing and photographing these images, it occurred to me that perhaps these aren't only for me. I made a commitment to share them in a book. That was a couple of years ago. I've been dragging my feet, letting everything else take priority, and now I'm grateful for the breakthroughs that have helped me get to this point. How often do I let fear and uncertainty rule the action, or inaction, I take in the world? How often do you?

I truly hope these images touch your heart as they have mine.

With Love.

I have included a few images from years long past because they still hold a powerful message for me, so I believe they deserve a place in this story.

Often in my wanderings and meanderings, I have noticed, and picked up heart-shaped rocks. Some of them sit on my altar. At the time, these were seemingly random discoveries to me, occurring sporadically over a period of months and years.

Now, as more and more hearts have continued to show up, I wonder just how random these earlier events really were. Is the world, creation, the Creator communicating with us all the time? Would the Creator offer a hagstone to remind me how magical this life is?

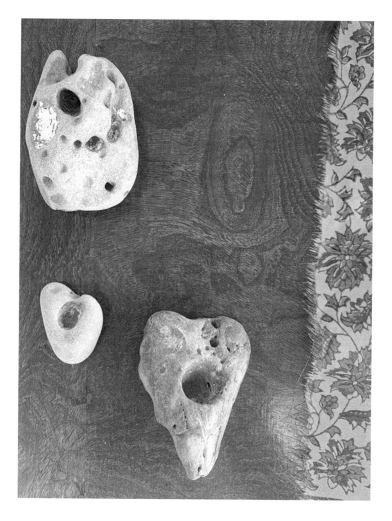

...."Hagstones are rocks that have naturally-occurring holes in them. The oddity of the stones has long made them a focus of folk magic, where they've been used for everything from fertility spells to warding off ghosts. The names for the rocks vary by region, but hagstones have been viewed as magical across the world.

A hagstone is created when water and other elements pound through a stone, eventually creating a hole at the weakest point on the stone's surface. This is why hagstones are often found in streams and rivers, or even at the beach.

Hagstones are known by other names in different regions. In addition to being called hagstones, they're referred to as adder stones or holey stones. In some areas, hagstones are referred to as adder stones because they're believed to protect the wearer from the effects of snake bite.

It's not uncommon to see people in rural areas wearing a hagstone on a cord around their neck. You can also tie them to anything else you'd like to have protected. It is believed that tying multiple hagstones together is a great magical boost, as they're fairly hard to find. Those lucky enough to have more than one should take advantage of the opportunity" ….*

Perhaps we are like the hagstone, in that the elements of life pound away at us, opening up a space in our hearts where more Love can reside.

*From Learn Religions, How Hagstones are Used in Folk Magic, by Patti Wigington, July 2019
https://www.learnreligions.com/what-is-a-hagstone-2562519

MOTHER NATURE

A walk in the woods

Sometimes the Love is a little rough and we may have to open our mind to see it. Sometimes we must shift our perspective to find the Love.

It is in Nature, I believe, where Spirit speaks to us most clearly. It is where the messages seem to be saying, "Look! I created this for your enjoyment!" My heart delights in this.

On that same walk in the woods with my husband, Richard. Follow his gaze….

Another fallen log

Leaf in our yard

Leaf on the West fork of the Washougal River

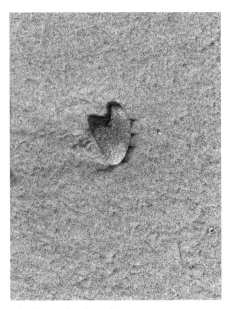

Shell on the beach

Tide pooling on the Oregon Coast with my husband, children, and grandchildren. I was feeling so much gratitude for this special time together. What a perfect time to see this heart formed in a beautiful tide pool filled with tiny sea creatures. Feeling the Love!

When I was young, I used to lie in the grass and gaze up at the clouds floating by and see what images I could find. That's still a wonderful way to spend some time, but I don't do it much anymore. I did not go searching for these cloud images. They came in the way all these images have come… in surprise and delight!

I remember a powerful time when I noticed that an image I was seeing "out there" in the world seemed to be a direct response to a question, a contemplation, a prayer. I was experiencing some conflict with a friend of mine. We had just had a difficult emotional exchange, and I went off by myself for a little while. I sat down in a field, closed my eyes, and asked, 'what am I to do here? How can I be at peace with this?' Shortly after that, I looked up in the sky. There, in a beautifully clear and bright blue sky, was a cloud formed in the shape of a heart. I don't have a photograph of it, but it is as clear in my mind's eye today, as it was in the sky those many years ago. It looked like a jet had flown in a heart-shape, leaving its trail behind to form the outline. At one point, the line was broken. The message came to me loud and clear:

KEEP YOUR HEART OPEN!

At the time I took a photo of this on my SLR camera. I looked and looked in my picture files and couldn't find it so I painted a picture to share the story with you.

WATER

Images from water that appeared as I was just going about my days....

At bathroom sink

In sink drain

On kitchen counter

On some fabricated material
in the shop

I spilled some water on the floor of our garage, grabbed an old blue towel, and wiped it up. When I shook out the towel to dry it, I saw this.

A painting project

A baking project

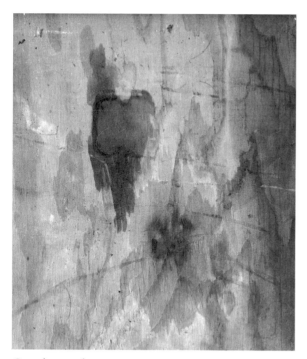

On plywood

On my sweatshirt

21

On the floor of the shop

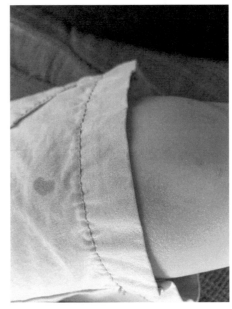

Grandson's pant leg

22

Doing the dishes, I left the ladle to soak. When I came back, this was waiting for me

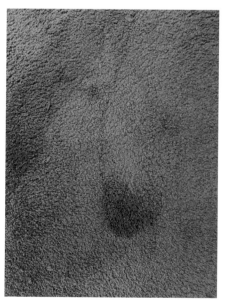

Spilled some of my tea, and this is what I found when I went to clean it up

AROUND THE HOUSE

I walked up to my front door one day, and my attention was called to a spot on the door

When I looked more closely, this is what I saw. I've finally stopped asking, how in the world did that get there? Now, I'm just saying, of course!

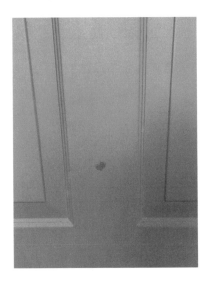

You know how sometimes it's difficult to get the first tissue out of the box? I finally ripped one out, and when I went back for another, I found this

Bandage stain on wound.
What!! Really?? Yes, really

Heart on sponge

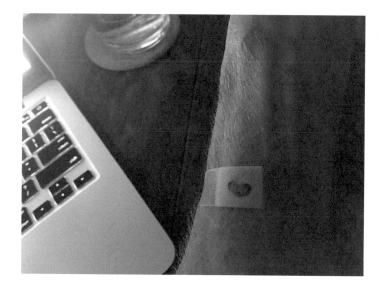

When my husband's parents died, we inherited their oak dining table. The table had taken a beating over the years. Its leaves were warped and stained. For several years, we used a tablecloth because it wasn't a pretty sight. A few years back, we had it refinished, and had three large leaves made to match so we could use it without a tablecloth and enjoy the beautiful wood.

I don't know how it happened, but a gouge appeared in the table one day. I know I would have been a lot more upset if the gouge hadn't looked like this! Love can be found everywhere! Even in the upsets.

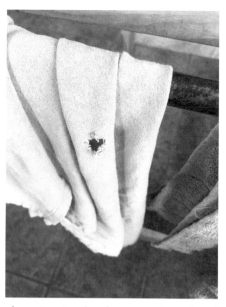

Hole in old towel. This was hanging in the shop one day when I went to clean up a project

Sweet little garden lava stone. Love from the fire.

Debris that fell out of Grandma Dorothy's
silver box when cleaning

Hair band on bath counter

My husband made this butcher block table for me about 40 years ago. A few years ago, I noticed this knot on one of its legs. What messages, what magic am I missing because I'm just not paying attention?

Hair strand on the bathroom counter

Owie from our goat, Boomer. He didn't mean it, but he can be a bit frisky at times

We were having a new deck put in, and the workmen were pulling out rocks and old plastic edging. I came out one day to talk to the crew and saw this.

I put a treat down for the dog in this little bowl. When I went to pick it up, the treat was replaced with this.

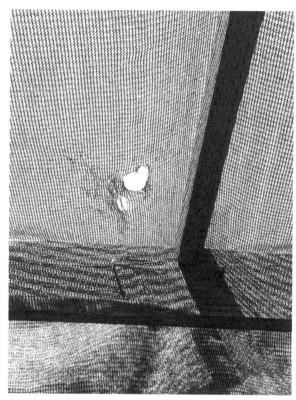

Tear in greenhouse shade cloth

A piece of tree bark on our gravel road

Lint in the laundry room

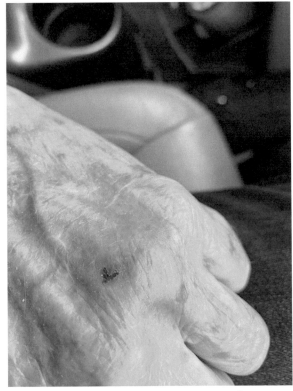

Another owie! Working on the farm, my poor hands take a beating. Notice how even the bruise under the scrape is in the shape of a heart. Behind it all is Love!

A piece of plastic wrap tossed aside. Later, I noticed this. Remember, I made a promise I would not manipulate any of these images as they showed up, and I have not

Rock step in the garden. The rock itself is not heart shaped. This image occurred when the soil and fine gravel from the path above washed down on to the rock. How much of the messy places in our lives have really been about creating space for more Love in our lives?

This heart on the gravel drive jumped out at me. If you look closely, you'll see that the actual rock isn't in the shape of a heart. It's the shadow that transforms it from an ordinary rock into a heart image. What parts of my own shadow do I resist? If I embrace my shadows, and have compassion for the aspects of me that are a little harder to accept, how much more Love would show up in my life?

FOOD

Of course, hearts would show up in the food and drinks we take in to nourish us!

ALL OF IT! The good and the seemingly Not-So-Good

What's not to love?

Moldy spot on a cucumber!

Poured some syrup in a bowl in preparation for some oatmeal. A sweet heart appeared!

Remember, I didn't make any of these images intentionally...

Picked up my morning cup of tea to wash it

Grandson's snack. It didn't look like
that when I gave it to him!

I scrubbed this egg, and the stain remained

Anyone who loves to make and eat ghee, knows why hearts would keep showing up here. It's so nourishing to the body. Ghee is created by removing milk solids from butter. It contains high concentrations of omega 3's. It's different from clarified butter in the way it is processed, on low heat, which maintains much of the nutrients!

PLANT LIFE

Spinach leaf

Dahlia petal

Bit of something on chard

Dogwood leaf

Collard green

Dahlia petals

OUT AND ABOUT

Walking path

Leaf on gravel path

Clearing & cleaning
Uncle Ed's house

Oregon beach

Cracked cement

New construction

On the road
(Photo contributed by daughter, Lindsay)

ANIMALS

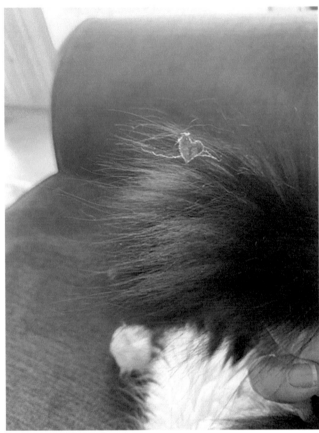

Our cat, Oliver. He jumped up beside me on the couch one morning, and this was on his tail

This is Max. He came to us when our 90 yr. old uncle could no longer take care of him. He was 1½ years old and had epilepsy. It is a challenge to take care of him. His medicine for epilepsy is expensive. He leaves me lots of slobber to clean up, and then he leaves me a heart made of slobber. He leaves lots of hair laying around to clean up, and then he leaves me a heart made of hair. I sometimes forget about Love and get grumpy and resentful. I'm noticing where I get stuck in resentment and forget to keep my focus on the Love that is right here in front of me.

Our cat Mister is no longer with us, but he was a sweetheart boy, as you can see

More Max slobber!

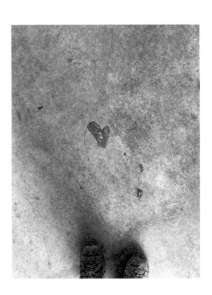

Our goat Radha, a gentle and sweet soul. If you're wondering where the heart is, you may have to squint to find it. I couldn't resist! Sometimes you do have to look a little deeper to find the Love!

Seriously? Yep…. This is some of the "ew" factor I mentioned at the beginning of the book. Just a little reminder that Love is present in ALL things…. Even in the kinda' icky stuff.

We give our dog, Max, medicine every single morning and night for his epilepsy. It gets a bit tiresome at times. He enjoys the canned dogfood that goes with the pills. I gave him his medicine one morning, turned back around to put the dogfood away, and this was waiting for me. I have no idea how that happened, but it felt like a sweet message of gratitude.

DHARMA THE COW

A Love Story

This is a Love story, perhaps just a bit different than most you've heard. It begins with our move to the country. We had sold our house in the suburbs, and on February 1, 2014, we moved to our new home.

In early March, Richard and I came home from running some errands and were greeted with this scene.

I phoned Bill, the neighbor who had cows, and told him we had a visitor who might belong to him. He came over and took her back to the pasture. A few days later, she was back, munching happily in our open pastures. I phoned the neighbor and said, "she's back!" and he came over and got her. He told me that he had checked the entire fence line, and said, "for the life of me, I can't figure out how she's getting out."

She showed up a couple more times, with Bill coming to get her, scratching his head about how she was getting out of his fenced pasture. One Saturday morning, I looked out my front window and saw this. I could almost hear her calling me out for a visit.

I decided it was time to take action and went outside for a chat. I told her that she really seemed to like it here, and I liked her being here so I would see what I could do. I phoned neighbor Bill, left a message telling him that she was back, that she seemed to want to be here, and I wanted to talk to him about her. A little while later, his wife called, and informed me that Bill had passed away. She told me, "That cow has never really bonded with the herd, so if you want her, you can have her." I offered my shocked sympathies and told her we would take her.

I phoned my husband, who was enjoying an early morning round of golf with friends, and told him, "We have a cow!" Then I drove to the local farm store and bought a water trough, a large grain bowl, some grain, and some hay. I named her Dharma because she seemed so clear about her purpose in life…. Eat, sleep, be free.

Dharma and I shared a fun greeting. When I would come upon her munching away in one of our open pastures, I would say, "Dharma, you're outstanding in your field." It always made both of us smile.

It's important to note that we had no barn, and no fenced pasture. Dharma roamed on our pastureland and woodlands freely. She particularly loved sleeping in the woods.

It's also important to note that about a month after neighbor Bill died, his wife sold the entire herd, perhaps to slaughter. I didn't ask. I can't help thinking that Dharma somehow knew she was going to be much better off with the two vegetarians who lived next door!

For five months, Dharma lived on our 27 acres, eating grass on the open pasture lands (and often in our lawn), sleeping in the woods, and truly being a free-range cow. She enjoyed hanging with the wildlife and not-so-wild life.

We lived happily this way, well, my husband wasn't too happy about the occasional cow pies in our yard! One day, Dharma disappeared. She was gone for about a week, and I was worried that something terrible had happened to her. Then, I got a phone call from another neighbor adjacent to us, asking if we had a cow. It seems Dharma had found their grasslands and apple tree. I walked over with a bucket of grain and coaxed her back home. Two days later she was gone again, and when I went back to the apple tree, she wouldn't follow me home.

I drove over to the nearby equestrian facility and put a note on their bulletin board, 'Neighbor needs help with runaway cow.' That afternoon I got a call, and a little later three riders on horseback met me at the apple tree and herded Dharma home. Since we still didn't have a fenced pasture, we got permission to take her back to neighbor Bill's pasture for the time being while we put in a small barn and fencing. She seemed happy to have the neighbor's entire pasture to herself and stayed put while we were in construction. This is Dharma in her new digs.

Dharma lived with us for close to two years, sharing the barn and fenced pasture with our goats, Laverne and Shirley. Though I believe she was happy, I have a sense she longed for those days of roaming free on the land and sleeping in the woods.

One day, Dharma got sick and stopped eating. The vet came out and told us she wouldn't recover. I took some more time with her, and after a couple of days I made the agonizing decision to call the vet back to euthanize her. Some friends came over with their backhoe and dug a very large hole in the pasture near the trees where she liked to be. I cried and said goodbye as the vet administered the drug. I couldn't watch her being put in the ground, so the goats and I came back later to pay our respects.

I put a lantern out on her grave because I couldn't stand the thought of her being all alone in the dark. It burned for three nights.

That was seven years ago, and I still miss her so much. My heart was truly broken open by the love, determination, and peaceful presence of this beautiful being. She wore the perfect "logo" on her back leg. I am so grateful for all you taught me about Love, sweet Dharma.

We buried Dharma on October 20, 2015. The hearts really started coming strong after she passed. They've been coming ever since.

The End and The Beginning

As Love Never Ends

Acknowledgements

As I said before, this book pretty much wrote itself. My job was to assemble and organize all the images and supply the narrative that went along with each image, and basically get beyond my uncertainties and fears about whether I could do this.

I sat on this project for a couple years, hemming and hawing, and spinning in circles about how to make this happen. I am so grateful to Jo Lynn Dow and Minda Redburn, two long-time and dear friends who have been the crew on my accountability boat. They have held my feet to the flames with a gentle, can-do attitude, and I know that I'd still be spinning if they hadn't been there to love and encourage me.

At a time when I was feeling particularly stuck about how to proceed with publishing this, I asked for guidance, saying, "Spirit, if you want this book published, show the way, because I have no clue about how to proceed." Not too long after that, my attention was drawn to a book that a friend published years ago. It had been sitting on my bookshelf for some time. It is Cherilyn Sunridge's book entitled, Nothing Is As It Was. I picked it up and thought that if my book could be even half as lovely as hers, I would be happy. Much gratitude to Cherilyn for leading the way, through the creation of her exquisite work, and for offering me much encouragement in my process.

Cherilyn's book was published by Balboa Press. The same afternoon that I picked up her book, I submitted an inquiry to Balboa Press, and the next morning I heard back from Melanie Foursha. She was so encouraging and enthusiastic, and she made the whole process sound full of ease. I knew immediately that this was the way forward. Michael March, at Balboa Press, has been very helpful in moving things along through the early stages of submission. Many thanks to you both.

It's a bit challenging to express the deep gratitude I have for my beautiful family. My husband, Richard, daughter, Lindsay, son, Evan, daughter-in-love, Hayley, and two amazing grandsons, Henry and Lou, are truly the best family one could wish for. You each contribute so much to my life through your constant and committed love and support. I am so thankful for this beautiful life we create together that is so much fun! I love you. Special thanks to my husband, Richard, and daughter, Lindsay, for helping to edit the draft of this book. Your insightful suggestions and on-going encouragement have been invaluable. A deep bow to Richard, for being my best friend and greatest supporter. I love the life we continue to build, encouraging each other in all that we do, and in who we are being, both individually and together.

Last, and very far from least, I want to express my deep gratitude to Spirit. You are the Author, the Supreme Messenger, and you are always showing us that Love is present in each moment. All we need to do is pay attention. For that I am eternally grateful, and utterly, completely in Love.

Printed in the United States
by Baker & Taylor Publisher Services